Through My Family's Eyes

By

Genise Brim

Table of Contents

This book is dedicated

to

The late Mrs. Estella Sarah Wesley Dailey

The mother who birth a legacy

The Bible speaks, in some translations, of the eyes being the light or window for the whole body. If all you could see was evil being done, this would bring nothing but darkness to the whole body. The eyes can be used to see that which is good, evil, harmful, or beneficial. That which we perceive affects our whole being.

When the African-American man was taken from his homeland, brought to a new land that was not his home, and forced to live in darkness and abuse. Darkness was the only thing a black man, woman, or child was forced to perceive. If the eyes see only darkness how great is that darkness.

….. if thine eye be evil, thy whole body shall be full of darkness. If therefore the light that is in thee be darkness, how great is that darkness Matthew 6:22-23 KJV

It was this evil that put darkness into the African American man.

Through
My Family's Eyes

Through My Family's Eyes

If someone asks me who the most inspiring person in our family is, I will say my grandmother, Estella Sarah Wesley Dailey. We (her grandchildren many are shown in the photo below) called her "Grandma Stella". Many times we would visit her and sit for hours laughing and receiving wisdom nuggets. She would always try to put money in your hand,

of course, many of us wouldn't take it. We would have sleepovers and laugh all night. Grandma Stella loved it when we took her to the beach. Any time she had a headache she always takes her all-time favorite regiment BC powder and a few sips of coke soda. In her ten decades of living, she has seen many seasons of change, but some things still remind her of the dark days of her youth. It is through her eyes that we will see glimpses of her life journey and the legacy she birth. It was January 2020, in Daytona Beach Florida where I visited my grandmother approximately two weeks after our family celebrated her 100th birthday. But after finding her birth certificate she is 103 years old. She sat in her wheelchair generally dressed in her pearls and a beautiful dress. But that day she was dressed very comfortably in her housecoat. I sat with her alone and she said these words to me… "I will tell you this"… I did not know what she was going to tell me, but she began to tell me what she remembered from her life story. So I began to write what she told me on some paper and the notepad on my phone.

Mrs. Sarah Wesley was born during the night in the back of a covered wagon, on January 19, 1917, in Bloxham, Leon county located in Tallahassee Florida. There is where her mother, Mrs. Elenora Wesley (our great grandmother) found work cleaning houses, and her father, Mr. Horace Wesley (our great grandfather) worked as a fisherman. Our grandmother Estella, said that her mother told her that when she was a baby, she would lay her in a box while she was cleaning houses. Her mother lived in a big beautiful house, which was one of the homes she cleaned and scrubbed floors. Mr. Horace was not allowed to live in the house with

them, he lived on a big boat that he used for fishing. The name of Mr. Horace's boat was "Lil Po Pete." The house

4

that both our grandmother and her mother lived in was owned by a man named Mr. Joe Taylor. Mrs. Estella described Joe Taylor as a man of an average height with a frame a little on the "heavy side" (she would say). His hair was long straight and black. His skin took on the appearance of a very bright-skinned man. Mrs. Estella was told by her mother that Mr. Joe Taylor was her grandfather, but he denies that he is her grandfather. However, her birth certificate shows that her mother's name is Nora Taylor, (Elenora Wesley our grandmother). Mr. Joe Taylor was an extraordinarily rich man, he had property, land, Studebakers, horses, racehorses, mules, and buggies. Although their lives seem to be well, they had troubled times. Life during the 1920s, for an African American, was hard and dangerous. Before the twenties, let us look back at the year 1919. It was branded "Red Summer" because of the bloodshed and one of the worst white-on-black violence in U.S. history. In America, the summer of 1919, ran red with blood from racial violence, and yet today, over 100 years later, not many people know it even happened. The bloodshed was the product of social forces: Black men were returning from World War

5

I, expecting the same rights they had fought and bled for in Europe. African Americans were moving north to escape the brutal Jim Crow laws of the South. Whites saw blacks as competition for jobs, homes, and political power. "Ethnic cleansing was the goal of the white rioters," said William Tuttle, a retired professor of American studies at the University of Kansas. They wanted to kill as many black people as possible and terrorize the rest until they were willing to leave and live someplace else. " The violence did not start nor end in 1919—some believe it started in 1917. Some count the era of Red Summer as beginning with the deaths of African Americans in East Saint Louis, Missouri, in 1917 and extending through the Rosewood Massacre of 1923. The trouble began when white men from several nearby towns lynched a black Rosewood resident and destroyed the black town in Florida. The Rosewood Massacre was based on unsupported accusations that a white woman had been beaten and possibly raped by a black drifter. All told, at least 1,122 Americans were killed in racial violence over those six years, stated by Tuttle's count. Mrs. Estella recalls this time during her life when she says she was about 6 years old. As she grew up in the servant house, Mrs. Estella states that both she and her mother seemed to have someone looking out for them. When they were in the main house, someone came rushing in telling them to go out the back door and get into a horse and buggy, because there were a group of white men coming to kill the black people in their neighborhood. Many black residents fled for safety into the woods. There were many times they had to leave the house, run across a bridge, run through muddy waters, to hide in the woods just to escape the angry white men. She states that there was a friendly white man that brought them food to eat while they were hiding. As she tells me this story, she begins to cry and say, she was so tired of running. One day when Mrs. Elenora was cleaning Joe Taylor's home, Mrs. Estella tells me that she was wearing a new white dress. She goes on to tell me of an incident that happened to her that day. At that time, she was about 8 years old. She was outside in the backyard when a white woman came out the door and threw black coffee on her white dress ruining it. She states that she knew she could not say anything because of the trouble she could face. Although they were treated with disrespect,

Mrs. Estella stated that Mr. Joe Taylor was kind to them and wanted to give Mrs. Elenora a house and a horse. Around this time she tells me her father had already died. She did not tell how he died. Maybe Mr. Taylor wanted to help them to become more independent. Nonetheless, Mrs. Elenora refused them all. But, Mrs. Estella had

wanted her mother to take those gifts. There is no date of when they moved or how they arrived in Armstrong, Florida.

Mrs. Estella only tells me that she and her mother migrated to Armstrong, Florida. When they arrived there, they had nowhere to live. For a short time, they lived with a lady that was willing to take them in. Mrs. Estella and her mother later started their walk to St. Augustine, Florida, which was thirteen miles. There is where they found work cleaning houses while living with another lady who took them in. Mrs. Estella did not talk much about her brother—she only told me that he died in a car accident in St. Augustine. While Mrs. Estella lived in St. Augustine,

Florida, she later married Mr. Alonzo Dailey, our grandfather and they had four children. The eldest, Gladys; Eugene; Geneva; and Yvonne being the youngest of the four. All of them were born and raised in St. Augustine, Florida. Unbeknown to her, she had birthed a legacy. Their father, Mr. Alonzo Dailey was enlisted in the US Army for several years. Mrs. Estella Dailey later separated from her husband because of his extramarital affairs. She never married again. Living in St. Augustine was not going to make their life any easier, because of its history which was a dark one.

The Dark History of
St. Augustine and the fight for
Civil Rights

The Dark History of St. Augustine and the fight for Civil Rights

S t. Augustine is known as the oldest slave trade marketplace and the first place in Florida where slavery started. This part of American history is not talked about much. The first black African slave arrived on the North American continent in 1565. The Spanish Pedro Menendez founded St. Augustine (was also known as Spanish Florida) on the northeast Florida coast. Pedro arrived with ships filled with families that were mostly African slaves. There was a 20-year occupation between St. Augustine and the British. They had slave ships regularly arriving either after stopping in the American colonies or coming directly in from Africa. St. Augustine is also where slavery ended. Fort Mose and the first underground railroad (north of St. Augustine) was established in 1738. It was the first black settlement in the

United States. Slaves from the British colonies that settled in Fort Mose were granted freedom. The slaves from the British colonies up north traveled the Underground Railroad, which headed not to the north such as the Carolinas, but south, to the Spanish colony of Florida and Fort Mose to be free. But the Jim Crow laws were passed in 1896, which kept African Americans from using the same facilities as whites.

Dr. Robert Hayling (right) Dr. King, Atlanta mayor Andrew Young. Photo by Frank Murray/Courtesy of The ACCORD Civil Rights Museum, St Augustine FL.

Segregation was now in the public schools, transportation systems, beaches, restrooms, and drinking fountains. Fast forward to the 1960s, the white people of St. Augustine, Florida were trying to have an annual day of celebration when it was described as the oldest community of the "White race only" in the U.S. So segregation was very prevalent in St. Augustine. Our grandmother Estella Dailey was not the only one who moved from Tallassee, Florida to St Augustine Florida. Dr. Robert Bagner Hayling moved to St. Augustine in 1960. Dr. Hayling, (later to be known as, the father of the movement) was the first black dentist in Florida to be elected to the American Dental Association. Dr. Hayling found the adult African Americans in St. Augustine to be complacent about racial discrimination. Many of the adults were in fear of losing their jobs and did not want to stir up more racial tension. Dr. Hayling joined the local NAACP in their protest of a segregated celebration of the city 400th anniversary, which described St. Augustine as the oldest community of the white race only in the U.S. The celebration takes place in front of the Old Slave Market Plaza now called The Public Market.

Slave Market Plaza is now called The Public market. Courtesy of The 40th ACCORD/St. Augustine RECORD Newspaper

It is true slaves are no longer sold in that market. But don't be deceived during the1960 the spirit of white supremacists persists along with the mindset of that which placed the slaves on that trading block. The hooded and unhooded mobster tries to reinforce the terror of those dark days onto the African American people of St. Augustine.

The young teenagers were more motivated to risk their lives to stop racial discrimination. Dr. Hayling organized the young teens into a Youth Council of the NAACP. He taught them methods of nonviolent activism. He arranged

picketing and sit-ins at white-only restaurants and wade-ins at a white-only pool and beach.

Courtesy of The 40ᵗʰ ACCORD/St. Augustine RECORD Newspaper

Because such segregation was still legally enforced, he was arrested many times along with local demonstrators and visiting supporters. Of the four children our grandmother Estella had, Ms. Gladys and Ms. Yvonne became demonstrators during the Civil Rights Movement. It is through their eyes we shall relive their story of the dark disgraceful customs of racial segregation in St. Augustine, Florida during the 1960s. Growing up in St. Augustine Florida was not easy nor was it safe for anyone of color. Ms. Gladys and her sister Ms. Yvonne had enough of the racial discrimination. But the spirit of hatred was not only found in the white race but also shown within their race. They took me back to the time when they were in elementary school. Each one told of a similar experience when they were in school. Their schools were segregated, the materials were low, books were tattered, and the school was plagued with abusive African-American teachers. Their principal and his sister would spank the student for any reason in their school. They said that the only way to get to school was to walk because the school buses were for kids across town, those on the north side, and the kids from out of town. Ms. Gladys and Ms. Yvonne talked about a cold day they walked to school—they stated that their feet felt like they were frostbitten. They also stated that if they would arrive late to school, they had two choices: stay outside and walk around the school while picking up the paper until the next class starts or get a beating and get locked in a black closet. Ms. Gladys stated that she hated school because they were always beaten with a piece of a big rubber tire. She added that the students were always mistreated. Some special students were given the privilege of writing down other students' names if they were caught doing something wrong. Some of these students would write down names of students that they did not like just to see them get in trouble. The names on the list would be given to the teacher and students would get a beating with a ruler on their hands or neck. Another complaint Ms. Gladys had stated was when she stays up all night to complete her homework assignment she would turn it in the next day to the teacher. The teacher would take it from her hand and throw it in the trash can. Ms. Gladys would say "from your hand to the trash can." She states that no student deserves this type of treatment from any teacher, especially being an African-American teacher. The school was not motivating Ms. Gladys at that time. Ms. Yvonne, the youngest sister says she was bullied in the first grade because she was so skinny. The students would call her "olive oil" and Pluto was her boyfriend. Ms. Yvonne recalls a time when a student that was an African-American girl, who also bullied her, stuck a pencil in her leg and the lead is still in her leg today, according to her. Her English teacher would hit her fingers with a ruler every time she misses a spelling word. This too made Ms.

Yvonne, like her sister Ms. Gladys, have reservations about school. She also experienced abuse in a school she went to, which was a house called 36. There, the teacher hit her on the shoulder so hard her shoulder would swell up. The teacher would beat the students until they were tired. Ms. Yvonne was afraid of the teacher. She said she was a student that didn't cause problems. You would think this would make these two girls have low self-esteem and become fearful and afraid. But during the 1960s when Ms. Gladys became a young adult she states that she had seen and been through enough abuse and segregation that she felt compelled to do something to make a difference in St. Augustine. Her younger sister Ms. Yvonne felt the same way but was too young to participate in some of the movements. Ms. Gladys and Ms. Yvonne recall a time when they were going to go to a civil rights meeting. But their grandmother told them not to go to the meeting at this time. Both were upset that their grandmother refused to let them go to the meeting. They later found out that the Ku Klux Klan invaded the meeting with acts of violence. The people that were in the meeting were beaten along with their leader, Dr. Hayling. Dr. Hayling was beaten and kicked badly, his jaw was broken, and they said that the KKK was trying to pour gas on him. They were glad that they weren't there. Their grandmother, Mrs. Elenora Wesley was a praying lady, and when she tells you something you better listen. St. Augustine was known to be plagued with Klansmen that worked in many plant companies and other businesses revealing their Klan's symbols. St. Augustine, during the 60s, was the oldest city still fighting the bitterly divided community on the North American continent. The African American people faced massive hostility which existed not only between the races but anyone who comes to bring a stop to segregation. There was a fear that fell on black men in the night when they tried to avoid the night threats of ambushes and sniper attacks. The negro leaders and followers lived with this fear for their lives. All the sit-ins, wade-ins, and other publicized demonstrations were done to integrate St. Augustine, Florida, one of the most segregated cities in the North American continent during the 1960s. Ms. Yvonne talks about a time when her sister, Ms. Gladys, and other picketers, including herself, heard that the KKK was going to march down Kings Ferry Way. This is where their other sister(my mother) Mrs. Geneva lived with her husband (my father) Mr. LeRoy Sumpter. Mr. LeRoy and Mrs. Geneva both lived with Mrs. Mozell Wise, (LeRoy's mother). Ms. Gladys, Ms. Yvonne, and the other picketers went to Kings Ferry Way to see the Klan march. Ms. Yvonne describes the march as she saw it. She saw white men covered with a white sheet with the eyes cut out and in their hands were chains dragging sticks and all kinds of things to bring harm to people, if anyone would leave off the side-walk. They watched the Klansmen walk down their street leaving to go to another street. But they didn't follow them. Ms. Gladys, Ms. Yvonne, and the others weren't intimidated because they were determined to get St. Augustine integrated. Ms. Yvonne recalls a time during the fourth of July when the city had fireworks displayed on the waters, but the black people were not allowed to come. Although Ms. Yvonne and her friends could not go where the fireworks were, they sat on a nearby ledge to watch. Also, one day when Ms. Gladys, her sister Ms. Yvonne and the other picketers were walking in a picket line, an elderly white lady spat on Ms. Yvonne while she and the others were singing and carrying a sign which read

"We Shall Over Come Because the Lord is on Our Side." They also sing a song, **"We shall overcome whites and blacks together, we shall overcome".** Ms. Yvonne stated that an elderly woman called her a "nigger" and said that all she was doing was wearing out her shoes. They were instructed by their leader not to fight back or say anything. Ms. Yvonne also stated that other white people would shout different derogatory words to all of them. Ms. Yvonne stated that they would tell them to go back to Africa where they belong so that they can live in peace. All the remarks they made did not stop them. They believed that their walking and protesting were not in vain. There were times when Ms. Yvonne had to run off the picket line and act like she was going to the restroom at the post office and stay there until the policeman left. The policeman would be checking for ID, and Ms. Yvonne was underage. But the next day she was back on the line sometimes with only three of them because they were determined to get justice for black people.

Photo Courtesy of Audrey Nelle Edwards/The ACCORD Civil Rights Museum, St. Augustine FL.

There were times Ms. Gladys and Ms. Yvonne put themselves in harm's way not knowing whether they would be hauled off to jail or beaten by the KKK. The thoughts of being hauled off to jail with a cattle prod and beaten with sticks filled their thoughts, but that did not stop them. They had a mother and a grandmother that prayed for them every time they left the house. They did not know whether they would return home dead or alive without police protection. Ms. Gladys is now married, and her name is changed to Mrs. Gladys McBean but she continues to fight for civil rights. When Mrs. Gladys, a few other young adults, and teenagers were going into a restaurant for a sit-in, they were asked to leave. In this restaurant, the people only served white people and refused to serve black people.

Mrs. Gladys and the others refused to leave. Therefore they were hauled off to jail, where they stayed for a month until Dr. Hayling came to bail them out. Mrs. Gladys was arrested three times: 7-18-1963, 8-13-1963, and 4-9-1964. One of the times Mrs. Gladys was in jail she shared a cell with a woman that hid a knife under her pillow at night. She states that they were told if we told anyone what she had, she would hurt us. We were in a cell with one toilet, one sink, with a shower with no curtain. Mrs. Gladys states that she slept on a tin bed with no mattress. She also state that she was exposed for everyone to see, so she slept in her clothes with no shower, because there was no shower curtain. She goes on to state that they made them go outside in the hot blazing sun to make them exercise. Mrs. Gladys states that the women would serve their food in a tin pan, they would not open the jail door, they would slide

it under the cell door on the floor. In the morning, Mrs. Gladys states that they would be served the better meal which was grits, bacon, egg, and water. But for dinner, they were served lima beans with fatback bacon, corn with bread.

Dr. King was arrested. Courtesy of The 40th ACCORD/St. Augustine RECORD Newspaper

Dr. Martin Luther King came to town and visited the church on Washington Street. Ms. Yvonne states that Dr. King was very polite, and he shook everyone's hands. Ms. Yvonne says his hands felt soft as cotton. On June 12, 1964, Dr. Martin Luther King Jr. was arrested on the steps of the Monson Motor Lodge when he asked to be served at a whites-only hotel restaurant.

In the following pages, you will see Mrs. Gladys McBean in a picture holding up a burned cross. Also, you will see her arrest record along with the transcript of the article "Nine Fined" describing her court day in session.

There were many months of bombing, burnings, and shooting in St. Augustine. Here is a picture of a burned house and Mrs. Gladys holding a cross used for burning.

Under cover of darkness, whites slink into Negro areas and burn crosses (l), and destroy homes (r) with deadly firebombs.

Here is a picture that captures Ms. Gladys holding up a cross used for burning that was found beside a burned-down house, in an African-American neighborhood. (Jet magazine November 21, 1963 Issue)

Gladys McBean Arrest Records

Gladys McBean Arrest Record

Courtesy of The ACCORD Civil Rights Museum/SJCSD, SJC, FL

DOB 5-20-40   4015

SHERIFF'S OFFICE, ST. JOHNS COUNTY, FLORIDA — CASE NO. 68343

Name McBeon, Gladys

Alias

Charge Trespassing after warning.

Address 443 W. 4th St., St. Augustine, Fla.

Description: Age 23   Sex F   Race N   Height 5'4"   Weight 105

Warrant from CJ   Arrested by C.P.D.   Date 8-31-63

Amt. of Bond $ 300.00   Posted 8-31-63   Highway Ins. Co. — Charles Cherry

Class Surety   Bond No. 51045

Return date 6-6-63   Court CJ   Disposition

Nolle Prosqui Case Dismissed   Date 12-6-63

Remarks

Fine Paid _____ Amount $ _____ Bond Est. _____ Amt. $ _____

Jailed _____ Report No. _____ Receipt No. _____ Date _____

SHERIFF'S OFFICE, ST. JOHNS COUNTY, FLORIDA — CASE NO. 67818

Name McBean, Gladys   Charge Trespassing   509.44

Alias

Address 443 W. 4th St., St. Augustine, Fla.

Description: Age 23   Sex F   Race N   Height 5'4"   Weight 105

Warrant from JP-9   Arrested by C.P.D. - Simson, D.S.   Date 7-18-63

Amt. of Bond $ 100.00   Posted 7-18-63   Class Highway Ins. Co. - Charles Cherry 51637   Surety   Bond No. 44278

Return date Subject to call   Court JP-9   Disposition

Remarks

Fine Paid   Amount $ Bond Est.   Receipt No.   Amt. $

Jailed   Report No.   Date

1-17 (Rev. 4-21-61)

UNITED STATES DEPARTMENT OF JUSTICE

FEDERAL BUREAU OF INVESTIGATION

WASHINGTON 25, D. C.

In Reply, Please Refer to
File No.

The finger impressions which have the number in individual finger blocks circled on the attached cards are not susceptible of accurate classification because of one or more of the various reasons listed below. Each fingerprint card indicates by number or notation appearing in the upper left corner the particular reason or reasons for its return.

(1) Ink was unevenly distributed.
(2) Fingers not fully inked or rolled
(3) Too much ink
(4) Insufficient ink
(5) Some impressions smudged, possibly fingers slipped while being rolled, or fingers not clean and dry
(6) Ridge characteristics not distinct, possibly due to the nature of the individual's employment or some other cause. Legible prints may be obtained after a few days.
(7) Hands have been reversed.

(8) One or more fingers printed twice
(9) One or more impressions missing or partially missing. Please indicate if there is an amputation. If no amputations, obtain these fingerprints. In cases of bent or paralyzed fingers, it is suggested that a spoon or similar instrument be used and the fingers be printed individually.
(10) Fingerprints not in sequence in spaces indicated
(11) Printers ink was not used. Other inks or chemicals are not usually legible or permanent.

Due to the volume of fingerprints contained in the fingerprint files of the FBI, and the use of super break-ups and extensions in conjunction with the Henry Classification System, it is necessary to obtain exact ridge counts and tracings of all ten fingers in order to search our files properly.

In the event of serious injury to a finger precluding the taking of prints of the finger at this time, it is suggested that printing be done at a later date when a complete set of prints may be secured.

It is suggested that reprints be obtained and forwarded to the FBI for appropriate attention. When submitting reprints it is not necessary to return the original fingerprint card, as only one copy of each set of fingerprints is necessary for retention in this Bureau's files.

For your information, a check by name only has been made on the enclosed prints with negative results.

Thank you for your cooperation in this matter.

John Edgar Hoover
Director

(over)

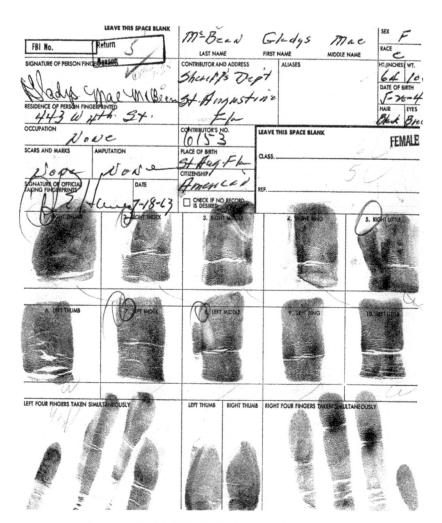

Courtesy of The ACCORD Civil Rights Museum/SJCSD, SJC, FL

In St. Johns

Nine Fined On St. Augustine Sitin Charge

By MABEL NORRIS CHESLEY
Associate Editor

ST. AUGUSTINE — With the sentencing yesterday afternoon for the second time, on charges stemming from racial demonstrations, the nation's oldest city is sinking deeper into its abyss of tension.

The nine were fined $100, or 45 days in jail for sit-in demonstrations at two local drug stores.

Previously four of them, Thomas Jenkins and Goldie Eubanks Jr., both 17, James S. Jackson, 18, and Francis Floyd, 20, were fined $100 or 30 days for distributing reprints of an editorial in the July 26 Daytona Beach Morning Journal.

Sentenced also yesterday were four more teenagers, James L. Jackson, Jerome Cliss, Gloria Thomas and Jimmy Pender, and Gladys McBean, 23.

Peace Justice Marvin Grier presided at the three hour trial.

It was highlighted by a burst of anger from Sheriff L. O. Davis over the disappearance of a letter he had written to the president of the Marion County Bar Assn. in Ocala, indicating cooperation with that city which also is suffering racial tension.

When the packed observer section of the courtroom—the great majority Negro — laughed at his anger, he ordered all of them out.

Grier previously had warned the spectators he would jam the courtroom if they interrupted the demonstration or prompted by his sentence of six of the young defendants. He was just starting the trial of the last three when the courtroom door burst open and the Sheriff shouted: "Who's got my letter?" The proceedings at the bench halted, and Sheriff Davis reached across several rows toward Dr. J. B. Hayling, the Negro dentist who is leading the St. Augustine desegregation movement, and demanded: "Come on, give me that later!"

It was handed over to him by a young Negro sitting beside Dr. Hayling.

When the Judge called a recess after the trial Sheriff ordered the laughing Negroes out. Davis was asked about the letter episode. "That was a personal letter, and I don't want it read by any one." He used the familiar term of derision for Negroes.

This writer, who had read the letter, asked what it was about.

"It's about a murder case I'm investigating, and they took it right out of my pocket," he fumed.

However, it was learned later that he had showed the letter to A. G. McCartney, one of the complaining lunch counter operators, who in turn passed it to a friend down the line. That man passed it on, and it fell into Hayling's hands.

The letter spoke of his hopes of getting a new law in the city to ban the silent parade of Negro pickets before places that bar them at lunch counters, and thanked the addressee for the advice that had been given previously.

Representing the Negroes at both of the trials was Earl Johnson, Jacksonville Negro attorney. He prodded the drug store owners to tell why they had had the demonstrators arrested, attempting to get them to admit that it was because they are Negroes.

The charges of trespassing were brought under a Florida statute which gives owners of such places the right to order any "undesirable" persons out, and lists causes of intoxication, boisterousness, uncleanliness and any who might cause the owner to lose business. All the defendants testified that none of the White people in the two stores left — in fact, James S. Jackson testified that some elderly White women came to their table and told him: "I'm glad you are here."

As Johnson prodded Whites with questions to show racial bias, the Peace Justice interrupted to order him to restrict his questions to whether they were in the places or not, and whether they complied with orders to leave.

In the audience, listeners began to stir, and there were angry murmurs.

St. Augustine's racial tension began last March and unwittingly was prompted by Vice Pres.

Johnson. He was to come to the city for a ceremony involving restoration of one of its ancient buildings, and the National Assn. for the Advancement of Colored People wrote and advised him of the tight segregation practices in the city. He informed the restoration planning committee he could not attend the banquet as conjunction with it barred Negroes.

Twelve Negroes were admitted to the banquet, and sat at segregated tables.

In the regulations that had been going on over the affair, Dr. Hayling said the NAACP had been promised a hearing by the City Commission on its grievances over official segregation practices the day following the banquet. A committee arrived at the appointed time, he said, to find only the City Manager on hand to hear them.

When that meeting failed to produce results, the NAACP heightened its pressure, and finally a meeting was held on a Sunday in May. Hayling said the Commissioners mostly declared that "Communists" or "the Manatees" were behind the Negro civil rights drive.

The dentist served as the main spokesman and the next day he was bombarded with telephone calls threatening his life. Shortly thereafter, a shooting incident occurred at his home and a Negro youth was shot in the heel. A group of White youths was arrested for the incident, but their cases were dismissed for lack of evidence.

In July, Negro youths began their demonstrations, and the arrests have included juveniles who were taken into the custody of the County Court because their parents refused to sign affidavits that they would not permit the youngsters to demonstrate until they were 21.

It was this practice that was criticized in The Morning Journal editorial. Negroes were arrested for delivering copies of the editorial at homes in an upper middleclass White neighborhood at the dinner hour one day last week.

Where does St. Augustine stand now?

The lines of resistance are tightening, and there is no communication between the races. The Police Chief, Virgil Stuart, like the Sheriff, is an ardent segregationist. He are the Commissioners. A state official in the city, who refused to be quoted on his views of the crisis, refuses to take his leadership, saying..."he can't afford politically, to get involved."

On the other side, the Negroes are growing more adamant.

Hayling, a Lieutenant in the Air Force before he became a dentist here two and a half years ago, says he will not give up until "my last dime is gone." He has put up bail money for most of the young demonstrators. One prominent White man said the dentist had been "sent here"—adding, "There are Communists in this thing, you know."

Hayling, a native Floridian, is a graduate of Florida A&M and Meharry Dental School, Nashville. He was commissioned from the ranks of the Air Force.

32

The Transcript of The Nine Fined Day in the Courtroom

(The above Article)

Permission was given, by Daytona New Journal

St. Augustine Sit in Charge By MABEL NQRRIS CHESLEY Asicclttft I-Mildred ST. AUGUSTINE -, With the sentencing yesterday afternoon of nine young persons, three for the second time, on charges stemming from racial demonstrations, the. nation's oldest city is sinking deeper into its abyss of tension. The nine were fined $100, or 45 days In Jail for sitting demonstrations at two local drug stores. Previously four of them, Thomas Jenkins and Goldie Eubanks Jr., both 17, James S. Jackson, 18, and Francis Floyd, 20, were fined $100 or 30 days for distributing' reprints of an editorial in the July 26 Daytona Beach Morning Journal. Sentenced also yesterday were four more teenagers, James

L, Jackson, Jerome Glass. Gloria Thomas and Jimmy Fender, and Gladys McBean, 23. Peace Justice Marvin Grier presided at the three hour trial. It was highlighted by a burst of anger from Sheriff L. O. Davis over the disappearance of a letter he had written to the president of the Marlon County Bar Assn. in Ocala, indicating cooperation with that city which also is suffering racial tension. When the packed observer section of the courtroom—the great majority Negro — laughed at his anger, he ordered all of them out. Grier previously had warned the spectators he would, clear the courtroom if they repeated the demonstration prompted by his sentence of six of the young defendants. He was just starting the trial of the last three when the courtroom' door burst open and the Sheriff shouted: "Who's got my letter?" The proceedings at the bench halted, and Sheriff Davis reached across several rows toward Dr. J. B. Hayling, the Negro .dentist who Is leading the St. Augustine desegregation movement, and demanded: "Come on, give me that letter!" It was handed over to him by a young Negro sitting beside Dr. Hayling. When the Judge called a recess after the irate Sheriff ordered the laughing Negroes out, Davis, was asked about the letter episode. "That was a personal letter, and I don't want It read by any —." He used the familiar term of derision for Negroes. This writer, who had read the letter, asked what it was about. "It's about a murder case I'm Investigating, and they took it right out of my pocket," he fumed. However, It was learned later that he had showed the letter to A. G. McCartney, one of the complaining lunch counter operators, who In turn passed it to a friend down the line. That man passed It on, and It fell into Hayling's hands. The letter spoke of his hopes of getting a new law in the city to ban the silent parade of Negro pickets before places that bar them at lunch counters and thanked the addressee for the advice that had been given previously. Representing the Negroes at both of the trials was Earl Johnson, Jacksonville, Negro. attorney. He prodded the drug store owners to tell why they had had the demonstrators arrested, attempting to get them to admit that it was because they are Negroes. The charges of trespassing were brought under a Florida^ statute which gives owners of such places the right to order any "undesirable" persons out, and lists causes to intoxication, bolsterousness, uncleanliness and any who might cause the owner to lose business. All the defendants testified that none of the White people in the two stores left in fact. James S. Jackson testified that an elderly White woman come to their table and told him: "I'm glad you are here." AS Johnson prodded Whites with questions to show racial bias, " the Peace Justice Interrupted to order him to restrict his questions to whether they were in the places or not, and, whether they complied with orders to leave. In the audiences listeners began to stir, and there were angry murmurs. St. Augustine's racial tension began last March and' unwittingly was prompted by Pres. Johnson. He was to come to the city for a ceremony involving restoration of one of its ancient buildings, and the -National Assn. for the Advancement of Colored People wrote and advised him of the tight segregation practices In the city. He Informed the restoration planning committee he could not attend if the affairs in conjunction with It barred Negroes. Twelve Negroes were admitted to the banquet, and sat at segregated tables. In the negotiations that had been going on over the affair- Dr. Hayling said the NAACP had been promised a hearing by the City

Commission on its grievances over official segregation practices the day following the banquet. A committee arrived at the appointed time, he said, to find only the City Manager on hand to hear them. When that meeting failed to produce results, the NAACP heightened its pressure, and finally a meeting was held* on a Sunday In May, Hayling said the Commissioners mostly declared that "Communists" or "the Kennedys" were behind the Negro civil rights drive. The dentist served as the main spokesman and the next day he was bombarded with telephone calls threatening his life. Shortly thereafter, a shooting incident occurred at his home and a Negro youth was shot In the heel. A group of White youths was arrested for the incident, but their cases were dismissed for lack of evidence. In July, Negro youths began their demonstrations, and the arrests have included juveniles who were taken into the custody of the County Court because their parents refused to sign affidavits that they would not permit the youngsters to demonstrate until they were 21. It was this practice that was criticized In The Morning Journal editorial. Negroes were arrested for delivering copies of the editorial to homes in an upper middle class White neighborhood at the dinner hour one day last week. Where do St. Augustine stand now? The lines of re-newed prejudice tightening, and there is no communication between the race. The Police Chief, Virgil Stuart, like the Sheriff, is an ardent segregationist. So are the Commissioners. A state official in the city, who refused to be quoted on his views of the clash, refuses to take the leadership., saying,he can't afford, politically, to get involved. On the other side, the Negroes are growing more adamant. Hayling, a Lieutenant in the Air Force before he became a dentist here two and r half years ago, says he will not give up until "my last dime Is gone." He has put up bail money for most of the young defendants. One prominent White man said the dentist had been "sent here"—adding. "There are Communists in this thing, you know." Hayling, a native Florida. is a graduate of Florida AAM and Meharry Dental School. Nashville. He was commissioned from the ranks of the Air Force.

This article and transcript can be found on the website: Civil Rights Library of St. Augustine

Permission was given, by Daytona New Journal

Many sacrifice their life and many put themselves in harm's way all for civil rights. It is through their acts that the Jim crow system of segregation was ended in St. Augustine Florida. The US Congress was debating civil rights legislation and the situation in St. Augustine Florida helped influence many lawmakers to vote in favor of the Civil Rights Act of 1964. President Lyndon B. Johnson signed the Civil Rights Act into law on July 2, 1964. This law outlawed employment discrimination on the basis of race, color, religion, sex, or national origin, required equal access to public places and employment, and enforced desegregation of schools and the right to vote.

Later Mrs. Gladys and her family moved to Daytona Beach, Florida where they continued to fight for civil rights. Her sister Mrs. Yvonne and her family, including their mother, and grandmother also moved to Daytona.

The Fight Goes On

The Fight Goes On

The fight still goes on into their children's generation. The following article will include Mrs. Gladys and Mrs. Yvonne's daughters. It is through their eyes we will relive their experience at Seabreeze Senior High. Shelia McBean (Mrs. Gladys's daughter), Cheryl, and LaShan Horn are both (Mrs.Yvonne's daughter), stood against segregation in their high school; Cheryl and her sister LaShan along with 60 others were arrested at Seabreeze Senior High School in the year 1983. The students were arrested and released the same day. Here is an excerpt from the article about what happened at Seabreeze Senior High in the year of 1983. The following excerpt is from the original article which was given *Permission by the Orlando Sentinel.*

Mrs. Yvonne Johnson and her daughter Lashan Harris

Lashan was one of the students at Seabreeze Senior High that was arrested during the stand against segregation in her school.

SEABREEZE SENIOR HIGH

News

IT'S TIME TO CORRECT INJUSTICE OF 1983

Bo Poertner of The Sentinel Staff

THE ORLANDO SENTINEL

April 15, 1995

It was described as an ugly year in the history of Seabreeze High School in Daytona Beach, Florida. Robert L Wheeler was the assistant principal responsible for student discipline. Mr. Wheeler was a white man accused by black students of favoring white students. The school had protests and counter-protest that divided the school campus. Sixty-six black students and four black ministers were arrested during one of the protests. Mr. Wheeler was reassigned to Mainland High School and the State Department of Education tried to take his administrative and teaching certificates. Mr. Wheeler's administrative charges included altering student grades, inducing teachers to change grades, transferring students from one course to another, also causing them to fail the first course, allowing students to leave campus, and favoring male athletes. *(Full article is with the Orlando Sentinel*

Twentieth Century

It is now the twentieth century, and many African Americans have reached multimillionaire, billionaire status, become CEOs of major companies, and many are middle-class professionals. We have also successfully had an African-American president—Barack Obama, a two-term president. Despite all these major milestones we still face injustice.

Voter suppression has risen again in the south and is rapidly spreading more abroad in our country. Not only that, but we are also experiencing modern-day lynching that is still being justified. We are fighting the senseless killing of our African-American men, women, and our young black men. Many African Americans lost their lives because of false accusations, such as Trayvon Martin, Breonna Taylor, Michael Ferguson, George Floyd, and many more. Many African Americans continue to experience unequal treatment by our justice system.

Just like Mrs.Gladys and Mrs.Yvonne fought for civil rights in the 1960s, we must continue to stand for what is right. God made all men equal and one day we all will stand before our Lord and give account for the deeds we have done, and no one will be able to escape that day. Let us continue to make a positive difference for the next generation.

Genise Brim (the author), the late Dr. Robert Hayling, and the late Gladys McBean

It doesn't matter which group stands for life, remember that all lives matter in the sight of God.

The fight continues…

Made in United States
Orlando, FL
23 April 2022

17131091R00029